Chris!

Be blessed by one or all of these poems.

Ed Shagott

From God's Heart, To Mine, To Yours

E.P. Shagott

WESTBOW
PRESS
A DIVISION OF THOMAS NELSON
& ZONDERVAN

Copyright © 2014 E.P. Shagott.

All rights reserved. No part of this book may be used or reproduced by any means, graphic, electronic, or mechanical, including photocopying, recording, taping or by any information storage retrieval system without the written permission of the publisher except in the case of brief quotations embodied in critical articles and reviews.

WestBow Press books may be ordered through booksellers or by contacting:

WestBow Press
A Division of Thomas Nelson & Zondervan
1663 Liberty Drive
Bloomington, IN 47403
www.westbowpress.com
1 (866) 928-1240

Because of the dynamic nature of the Internet, any web addresses or links contained in this book may have changed since publication and may no longer be valid. The views expressed in this work are solely those of the author and do not necessarily reflect the views of the publisher, and the publisher hereby disclaims any responsibility for them.

Any people depicted in stock imagery provided by Thinkstock are models, and such images are being used for illustrative purposes only.
Certain stock imagery © Thinkstock.

ISBN: 978-1-4908-6370-2 (sc)
ISBN: 978-1-4908-6371-9 (e)

Library of Congress Control Number: 2014922369

Printed in the United States of America.

WestBow Press rev. date: 12/16/2014

Perfect World

I tried to envision a perfect world
where everyone would be free.
A world without suffering and pain
where all lived in harmony.

A world without bitterness.
A world without shame.
A world without differences.
A world without blame.

Never having to say you're sorry
for you never did any wrong.
A world filled with laughter.
A world filled with song.

Could there ever be such a place?
Yes, for it is in God's plan.
We would all be there now
if not for the fall of man.

So people don't get discouraged
remember to think before you do.
Until we get to our "Perfect World"
this one will have to do.

I Need Your Help Today, Lord

I need Your help today, Lord,
for it seems I can't go on.
Everything in my life today
appears to be all wrong.

The beauty that You created for me,
my eyes are failing to see.
There is disease throughout my body, Lord,
that is slowly killing me.

My smile seldom appears now,
overtaken by grief and pain.
My spirit is slowly being broken,
Lord, please touch my heart again.

May my focus always be on You, Lord,
so my problems seem far away.
Thank you for this time Lord
Yes, I need Your help today.

God's Wounded

With bones that are frail
and muscles that are weak,
God's wounded look for answers
and comfort they seek.

With movement that is limited
and not many places to go,
God's wounded days seem longer
filled with boredom, you know.

With eyesight that's failing
and hearing that's lost,
God's wounded look for something
which is found at the cross.

For life still has meaning
and still precious you see,
for God's wounded now need help,
they need you and me.

Someday you might be wounded
and be looking above
now one of God's wounded
you'll also be, looking for love.

Gifts

Each breath I take
each sunrise I see
each sound I hear
are gifts from Thee.

Everything I touch
every step I take
more gifts for me
that my Lord did make.

A forgiving heart
a caring way
a truthful nature
yes, more gifts each day.

Every smile I make
every laugh in fun
every hand I'd shake
every friend I've won.

Food to eat
and water to drink
all gifts from You, Lord
which makes me think.

The reason for all these gifts
is now so plain to see
because the greatest gift of all
is just Your love for me.

I Try

I try not to cry
when I feel sad.
I try not to get angry
when I am mad.

I try not to show pain
when I'm at my worst.
I try to hide my emotions
whenever I am hurt.

But now and then
the tears do come,
my anger when there
I know hurts someone.

The pain in my body
is sometimes so strong
I feel in this world
I just don't belong.

So what I can do
to make each day the best
is focus on Jesus
when I face each of these tests.

I can think of how
He suffered for me
so long ago
on a hill called Calvary!

You Were On My Mind Today

You were on my mind today,
for reasons I am not aware.
So I stopped and asked the Lord to be with you
and to give you His special care.

I asked Him to tend to all your needs
and give you strength if you feel weak.
I asked Him to listen closely to your heart,
for all the answers that you may seek.

I mentioned how special a friend you are,
then realized, that He already knew.
For when he looks into my heart
He sees a place marked just for you!

So I know my prayer will be answered,
as I give thanks to our Savior above.
And I know you will be blessed today,
all because of His unselfish love.

I Love You, He Said

I love you, He said,
as the first nail went in.
I do this for you
because of your sin.

The shame that I bear
I do this for you,
He said this as
the mallet hit nail number two.

The reason I came
was so all would be free.
I love you, He said
as they hit nail three.

He hung there for hours,
then bowed His head.
"My Father, why have You forsaken me?"
"I love You", He said!

It Was Never About This Life

It was never about this life
never was, never will be.
For it is not about you
and is not about me.

This short life of ours
Has meaning very true,
it is all about love
His love for me and you.

For we needed time to learn
He knew we just wouldn't understand,
by faith we must believe
that there is a promise land.

A land called grace.
A land filled with love.
A home He created for us
where Christ waits above.

A home where there is no sin
no guilt, no shame.
A home where we all live as one
and "Love" is our last name.

So each day you are on this earth
think how blessed you have been.
For you have one more day
to learn it's all about Him!

When Words Just Aren't Good Enough

When words just aren't good enough
to get you through your day,
I prayed to the Lord up above
to please show me another way.

I asked Him what could I do
to help take the darkness out?
He answered, "My child, that is My job,
as long as there is no doubt."

He said to this heart of mine,
"To family and friends always be true.
Comfort and healing comes from Me,
the friendship comes from you.

Always try to be understanding
as your day comes to an end,
that just lifting them up to Me
is the best part of being a friend."

So I hope knowing all this helps
when these days seem so long and tough.
Because sometimes you will need something
when words just aren't good enough!

I'm Talking To You

Why are you so down?
What can it be?
I raised my eyes above and asked
"God, are You talking to me?"

He said, "Everything that is,
and all you see,
was made just for you
and it all comes from Me!

The blood I shed,
the tears I cry,
are all for you
and still you doubt, why?

All I ask,
since you don't seem to see,
is that someday you will choose
to believe in Me!

My Word was left
so you would know,
I am always here
and love you so!

So don't be so down
and to My Name always be true.
Yes, my child,
I'm talking to You!"

I Want To Be Like Him

I walked into a room today
and made someone smile.
This person looked up at me
and said "Please stay for awhile".

She told me it has been so long
since anyone seemed to care,
and how grateful they were
that I took my time to share.

Yes, it seems everyone is so busy
even family and friends of mine.
Too busy thinking of themselves,
pretending there is no time.

This person asked me why I do it
and to His mission I stay so true?
I said, "Because I want to be like Him,
isn't this what Jesus would do?"

May This Day

May this day be about You, Lord,
may my thoughts be of You.
May each action that I take, Lord,
be just like You would do.

May I strive to be less selfish,
may my words just come from You.
May my life be a living sacrifice
in all that I do.

May each person that I meet
may I plant a tiny seed.
May it nurture in their heart, Lord,
and bring them closer to You indeed.

May they understand as I do,
may their hearts be filled with love.
May this day be about You, Lord,
as we give praise to our Savior above.

The Heart

The heart is very interesting
its job is so immense,
for it to fail is not an option
through days that are intense.

It also holds emotions,
those good and also that are bad.
It has to work so much harder
on the days we feel very mad.

Of all the places in us
that God chose from above,
He chose the heart for His Spirit to live
and work through Christ's precious love.

So when you're feeling troubled,
in your heart His Spirit seek,
and listen very carefully
to the Word that He does speak.

But if we do not listen
from the heart what the Spirit has to say,
we find the heart gets very exhausted
just to make it through the day!

The Warrior

The battle was on going
it never seemed to end,
but the warrior stood firm
always fighting and never giving in.

One enemy after another
each one trying to bring defeat,
but the warrior never quit
knowing victory would be complete.

Each separate battle that was fought
brought hurting of its own,
each enemy solider seemed determined
as the warrior stood alone.

When will this battle be over?
How long must the warrior fight?
When is enough, really enough?
Is the end of the battle really in sight?

For the answer to these questions
the warrior must look above,
see the battle was already won,
Jesus proved this through His love.

Our earthly battles will always be
John 16:33 said it so,
yes, the final battle the Christian warriors win
it was won over 2000 years ago.

So keep fighting Christian soldiers,
the victory will be done,
not on earth but in Heaven
when Jesus smiles and says, "Warrior, well done!"

Please Let Me Use

Please let Me use your heart,
the one that you gave to Me,
so all my wounded children can feel
the love that they desperately need.

Please let Me use your eyes
so from My Word you can read.
Teach them what was written
and just how important it is to Me.

Please let Me use your hands,
to reach out and touch for Me,
to hold My children ever so close
for that's so important for them, you see.

Please let me use your time
before it all runs out.
Please let me use your being
for that's what it is all about!

The Morning Of September 12th

It was the morning of September 12th,
something was different indeed.
A piece of every American,
was missing and we no longer felt free.

The churches became full again.
Many cried out to God.
Many probably blamed Him,
because they were so mad.

How could God let this happen,
probably so many did ask?
But His children knew the answer,
it was man's choice, like all the rest.

Now also in that morning,
if you listened to Heaven above,
3000 plus souls were returning home
and once again surrounded by His love.

So to all of us that were left behind,
our job is still so great.
We must tell everyone about God,
before it is too late!

Touch Someone For Me

As I awoke this morning from sleep
and my eyes opened to see,
the Lord spoke to my heart and said,
"Touch someone for me!"

He said, "Tell someone that I love them,
and if you follow my commandments you will too,
please touch someone for Me today
before the day is through!"

So as I started on my way,
I saw someone that was in need.
I said, "Is there something I can do for you,
what is it, please tell me, what can it be?"

The person looked me in the eyes
and said, "Why do anything for me?"
I smiled and said, "Because I was in need one day,
and thank God, someone took their time, you see!

See God spoke to my heart today
and brought me here just for you.
Because of His love for all of us,
He knew just what you needed too."

So listen ever so carefully, my friends,
when God tells you what to do.
For when He says, "Touch someone for Me,"
It's about Him, and not about you!

Planting Seeds

I am His little gardener,
whom God chose me to be.
He said, "Little gardener of Mine,
go plant these love seeds for Me."

I said, "Lord where do I plant
these seeds of Your love?"
God said, "Just listen to your heart,
as I speak to you from above.

Do not be surprised
if rejected now and then,
these seeds are the beginning
that will spiritually nourish them to the end."

So I reached deep into my heart,
and grabbed one of His special love seeds.
From my mouth they were planted as I said,
"This is from God's love, and also they are from me!"

I Am Someone Special

I am someone special
for all the world to see,
but when you look upon my face,
you are not really seeing me.

The face that you are seeing,
is the person I want to be.
I want to be like Jesus,
for my Lord and Savior is He.

So when you look into my eyes,
may they reflect His love indeed.
May my mouth speak His Words of love,
that have set so many free.

May my ears be always listening
for those worse off than me.
May my hands reach out as Jesus would,
to help all those in need.

May each person that I meet
as I travel on my way,
tell someone in their lives,
"I think I just saw Jesus today!"

New Through Christ

Ever since the day I was born
my life was not my own.
It had a purpose to fulfill
until He calls me home.

But what is always most troubling
as each day I strive to live,
is understanding it is not about me,
but to all the others that I must give.

It is not about my accomplishments,
but instead what Christ has done for me.
I am no longer of myself,
because Jesus set me free.

He freed me from this worldly sin,
which is upon us day and night.
As His sinless body hung nailed to the Cross,
that made me special in the Father's sight.

My days are all for Him now,
my burdens are oh so few.
I am this righteous child of God
through Christ, I am brand new.

God's Gift

Think of all the wonderful gifts
that you have already received.
How can anyone of them compare
to God's gift, once you first believed?

It will never be out dated,
nor decay as the years pass by.
The gift of salvation is for you and me,
just because of God's love, we didn't even have to try.

A gift to last forever,
just because we are His.
A gift that was paid in full,
oh what a special gift it is!

So remember to say "thank You",
every morning, noon, and night.
The only person to give a gift like this
is Jesus, because He definitely has the right!

Grab Hold

I started to fall
and didn't know why.
I needed help
and started to cry.

I looked around
for someone to see.
I started to yell,
please, someone, help me.

I looked to my left
and then to my right,
my worst fear was known,
there was no one in sight.

No one to my back
or to my front,
I couldn't walk
and I couldn't run.

I cried out to the Lord,
where are You to behold?
He said, "Lookup, My child,
and just grab hold!"

Modern Day Disciple

I am a modern day disciple,
for Jesus has chosen me.
Ever since my very first breath,
He has been waiting patiently, you see.

Jesus said, "Do you really love Me?
Would you give up everything you love?
Can you leave it all behind because I asked you to?
Giving praise to the Father above!

Can you love your fellow man
more than he does of you?
Are you willing to lose it all,
just because I asked you to?"

I said, "Lord, You know my heart,
with You I long to be.
Thank You for always asking,
"Modern day disciple, come and follow Me."

Whispers Of Love

God whispered in my ear today,
and the sweetest sound it was.
He said, "I love you, child of Mine",
as the angels sang above.

Sweet words of love, oh so true,
that just melted in my heart.
He whispered, "I am always here for you,
for you were special from the start."

Then He whispered, "I have whatever you need,
for with my love you never will lack.
All I ever wanted, My child,
is that you love Me back."

I felt a warm feeling
as His whispers warmed my soul.
I said, "Lord, You are my life now,
because I love You so!"

Being Humble

I am a humbled person,
when my eyes are on someone, but not me.
I am humbled in the presence
of someone longing to be free.

I am so very humble,
when I see the hurting and the lost.
I am also humble
in the presence of Jesus and the Cross.

See, the reason this makes me humble,
is because God opened my eyes to see.
If not for His love and grace,
there never would be a me.

It is nothing I ever did,
or could ever hope to do.
It is because He looked down from above
and said, "I love you!"

Are You Ready

I heard a knock on my heart,
it was Jesus calling me.
He said, "Child of Mine, are you ready to come home
or do you want Me to let you be?

Do you still want to stay
in this world filled with sin?
Are you ready to come home, My child,
Heaven is ready for you to enter in!"

I said, "Lord, my bags are all packed
and with You I want to be,
but there is still so much to do here,
and so many longing to be free.

I have many friends and family,
that don't know You like I do.
I want them to be in Heaven with me,
before their life on earth is through.

So whatever time You give me,
it will always be devoted to You.
Sharing Your love with others,
so they can be in Heaven too!"

The Key

As I walked up to the Kingdom gate
I couldn't enter in,
for it was locked and very secure
and the lock was titled "sin"!

I knew the place I wanted to be
was on the other side,
but my sin was keeping me from getting there
and also my foolish pride.

The Kingdom gate was too high
for me to try and climb.
It's lock was too heavy to break,
no matter how hard I tried.

Then in my heart I heard a voice,
it was very personal to me.
Jesus said, "The only way is to believe,
for I Am the Living Key!"

It was then that I finally understood
the only thing I could do,
is put my life in Jesus hands,
for only He can get me through!

Fruit From The Cross

Who would of thought
that something so sweet,
could come from a tree
where Jesus died for you and me.

A tree that was used
to bring suffering and shame,
to the Son of Man
and Jesus is His name.

But from that tree
His fruits began to live on.
It took His unwavering love,
before it all began.

So praise to God the Father,
for on that tree His Son paid the cost.
It was the only way that through us,
we can bear fruit from the Cross!

Your Purpose

You have a job to do for God,
something you were designed to do.
So many people go through life
never understanding what theirs is too.

The work that He has for us,
to many may seem simple or small.
But to God, our Father above,
important work for one and all.

See, the more you focus on Jesus,
you'll understand the work He has begun,
for He always said, "Father, not my will,
but let Your will be done!"

Friends, you will never understand your purpose
that God created you to be,
until you can look in the mirror
and say to yourself, "It's not about me!"

Crosses

I had a dream I walked with Jesus,
carrying our crosses, side by side.
Though mine was so much smaller,
I felt Him lift the burden as time went by.

With each step He looked at me,
His eyes were filled with love.
He steadied me when I began to stumble,
giving praise to the Father above.

At first the journey seemed too long,
to carry my cross all that way,
Jesus spoke to me and said,
"It's not about the burden
but what you do through it today."

So whatever the cross you are carrying,
may it become an aide to you,
to help someone else that is hurting
and show them Jesus is with them too.

He Is Always There

I reached my hand out to Him,
I felt Him grasp my heart,
His love grew even stronger,
than when my walk with Him did start.

I cried out "Thank You, Lord Jesus",
for He always hears my call.
He is always there for me,
if I stumble or even when I fall.

He loved me before I knew Him,
He is there day by day.
I cannot live without Him
for there is no other way.

And what is truly amazing
is if I feel like this today,
I can't begin to imagine how it will be,
when Jesus and I will be together some sweet day!

The Christian Hurts

The Christian hurts like everyone else,
we feel the suffering and the pain.
But what separates us from all the rest
is the power of Jesus name.

When storm clouds come
and the sun disappears,
we can stand firm,
for with Jesus we have no fear.

Though the pain is real
and the suffering is there,
our Lord and Savior gives us
no more than we can bear.

So stay firm on His Word,
and to His name always be true.
For because of His love,
He is always there for you!

The Lonely Road

I am traveling a lonely road
where others have also been.
But every time I travel this road,
it's filled with sadness and despair again.

How can I change direction?
Which way is actually right?
I am so tired of being in darkness.
Can someone show me where is the light?

I hear a voice in the distance
Saying, "Come to Me, even though you cannot see.
I am your Lord God,
come to Me and really be free.

Whatever obstacle you encounter,
I have conquered before you.
Keep walking toward the light,
for you will find Me there, too!"

"d"epression Came To My House

"d"epression came to my house
and said, "I think I'll stay a while.
One of the many tasks I'll do
is take away all the smiles.

I will rob them of their happiness
and take away all their joy.
It will not matter who it is
either a girl or a boy.

The longer they let me stay,
the harder it will be for me to leave.
I will take away all their pride
and in failure they will believe."

But I said, "Not so fast there little "d",
with me you will not tame,
and for all others in this house
I claim them in Jesus name.

Right now you may think your winning,
but soon I know you will lose.
The victory is in Jesus Christ,
once all the others decide to choose.

I Took It All For Granted

When I awoke this morning,
from my eyes I could not see.
The light that once shown from the window,
it's now all darkness to me.

I tried to call out for help,
but my words they would not flow.
The blessings I took for granted yesterday,
are no longer with me now.

My limbs that once were active,
now hang limp at my side.
My feet that once carried me to places,
are not responsive, even when I try.

The moral of this poem is,
"Do not take for granted what you have today,
use what the good Lord has blessed you with,
for His purpose, before it goes away."

A Dad Entered Heaven

A Dad entered Heaven,
Jesus met him at the gate.
Like all other Dad's, he was right on time,
for no one enters Heaven late.

Jesus said, "Dad, what is it that you did
on earth with your time?"
The Dad looked up at Jesus and said,
"The best I could of what was mine.

I tried to love my wife,
with all the love I had.
I did the best for my kids,
though sometimes they made me mad.

I worked hard every day,
sometimes longer than I should.
I wanted to provide for my family,
the very best way that I could.

But now what I understand,
what was most important to me,
is that they love You like I do,
so together, we once again can be."

Wings

The burdens of life are many,
trouble and heartache has come our way.
I raised my eyes above and said,
"Lord give us wings to fly away!

Please let my wings take me
to a place that's safe and free,
Free from life's constant battles
that are always all around me."

Within a few moments
I felt God's presence, oh so near.
Jesus spoke to my heart and said,
"Why is it that you fear?

If I give you wings they will lift you up,
but in this world troubles will always be.
It is not the wings that will free you from them,
but the faith that you have in Me!"

It's Up To You

It's up to you what you do,
the choice is totally yours.
You decide each step you take
as you walk throughout your years.

Right or wrong, good or bad,
you decide what to do,
but as you decide always remember,
God is watching you.

You can make someone happy
or take away their smile.
The words that you choose to speak
can make or break them for a long while.

You can decide to forgive,
the wrong someone has done,
or you can harbor resentment,
right from the beginning of day one.

The choice is yours given by God,
for that's the way He wanted it to be.
Ever since the fall of man He said,
"You can choose a sinful life or you can choose Me!"

Show Them, Touch Them, Reach Them Lord

Show them Lord of Your awesome power.
Touch them Lord with Your mercy and grace.
Reach them Lord so they all will know,
 it's not about this time or of this place.

Show them Lord that Your Word is truth.
Touch them Lord so they will never stray.
Reach them Lord each click of the clock,
 for it's not about them, but You each day.

Show them Lord each stripe on Your back.
Touch them Lord so they will finally understand.
Reach them Lord as only You can do,
 for You truly are the Great I AM!

Show them, Touch them, Reach them Lord,
 so in their lives You become so true.
Use me Lord to show, touch and reach them,
 so they all can love You, like I do!

The Son's Light

Don't walk in darkness,
when His light is always there.
Let Jesus brighten your day
and take away your despair.

Don't let the worries of today
keep dark clouds all around.
Step out into the Son's light,
and see all His beauty to be found.

Don't listen to the worldly lies
that bombard us every day.
Let the Father, Spirit and the Son's light
shine through you today.

Do trust in the Heavenly Father
as you go throughout your day.
Believe in His Word and be blessed
and let His Son light your way.

The Eyes Of The World

The eyes of the world are upon us,
as we go about our day.
The eyes of the world are upon us,
watching what we choose to do today.

What we show to everyone around us
demonstrates what we truly believe.
The eyes of the world are watching
and God is also watching you and me.

Be careful of the choices you make,
please think before you speak.
Remember what Jesus said,
"What you do to someone you are also doing to Me."

So as you go throughout your daily journey,
be careful what you do and say.
It can make the difference in someone's life,
if they see Jesus in you today!

An Alphabetic Poem To God

An **A**bundant life for us You give,
with all the **B**eauty that there is.
Always **C**aring for each of us,
as a Father **D**evoted to His kids.

Everlasting home You prepare for us,
because You're **F**orgiving of our sins.
A gift because of Your **G**race,
Your our **H**ealer and our friend.

Always **I**nterested in all we do,
Jealous if another god we choose.
Kindness You always pour out to us,
Loving no matter what we do.

A **M**ighty God You definitely are,
Never far and always **N**ear.
Over and over forgiving us,
with a love so righteous and **P**ure.

You never **Q**uestion what we do,
just **R**eassuring us along the way.
Staying close by our sides,
showering us with **T**ender mercies every day.

The **U**ltimate price You did pay,
With a **V**alue that stirs within.
You are truly the **W**orthy One,
that **X**-ed out all our sin.

Praise to You, Heavenly Father,
may our hearts always **Y**earning to be,
sharing our love and **Z**eal,
with You throughout eternity!

The Rivers Of Grief

The rivers of grief can run so deep,
it's waters are so icy cold.
We wait and wait for relief,
and for some comfort to behold.

Hour by hour, day by day,
when will our sorrows end?
Grief's currents are so very strong,
not giving way for family or friends.

Then within all my struggles,
God's voice became so crystal clear.
He said, "Do not be discouraged child of Mine,
but look for a lesson to be learned here.

See grief will come and grief will go,
it's all just a matter of time.
Look for the wisdom that lies within,
remember it's not in your time, but Mine."

Reach Into God's Toolbox

When life's problems get overwhelming,
and a solution you're looking for,
reach into God's toolbox
to solve this problem and more.

If the devil gives you heartaches,
filled with jealously, anger and hate.
Reach into God's toolbox,
to fix the problem before it's too late.

Grab onto the tools from the Spirit,
love, joy, peace, and patience, just to name a few.
So whatever the devil is throwing your way,
God has the right tool waiting for you.

Remember the devil wants to keep you discouraged,
thinking each day you will always lose.
God has given us victory through His Son,
all we have to do is choose!

The Ashes of Life

God reached into my ashes
and grabbed onto what was there.
It contained many of my hopes and dreams,
the remains from my anger and despair.

He held them gently in His hands
and caressed them with His tears.
He said in a loving, tender voice,
"these ashes are Mine, along with all your fears."

Then God whispered to my heart,
"Listen to my Spirit and from My Word take heed.
I have everything you will ever want,
I am all you will ever need!"

I lifted my eyes to Heaven,
and thanked the Father above,
for through the ashes of my life,
He created beauty, all because of His love.

Here I Am Again Lord

Here I am again Lord,
praying on bended knee.
So many issues in my life
that are really bothering me.

I want to be healthier,
though I don't eat like I should.
I want to have more money,
but wouldn't work for it if I could.

I want to have more friends,
though I don't talk to the ones I have.
I want my family to love me more,
but when I'm with them they make me mad.

So God I am still waiting,
for You to answer my prayer,
and if You decide not to,
well, I think it's not very fair.

Now the moral of this poem is
unanswered prayer we're always asking why?
See, God is waiting to bless us,
once the focus is off the "I"!

The Edge Of Heaven

God walked over to the edge of Heaven,
and then looked down at me.
He said to His many angels,
"See that one, he is special as can be!

Every time I look into his heart,
I see his love for me shining through.
Because he believes in My Son, Jesus,
he also believes in Me too."

So as all the angels looked down
from the edge of Heaven above,
the Father gave them instructions
to protect me, and shower me with their love.

"Steady him if he stumbles,
pick him up if he falls,
Holy Spirit, listen to his prayers,
and tell Me when he calls."

Then from the edge of Heaven,
God looked down at all the rest.
"Because of their love for My Son Jesus,
they truly will also be blessed."

Christ Lives Within Me

Christ lives within me,
our lives are now as One.
He was the One who has chosen me,
ever since the world begun.

Ever since the Garden of Eden,
when He created Brother Adam and Sister Eve,
He knew I would also be special to Him,
all I had to do was just believe.

He is an awesome God,
Who reigns from the Heavens above.
A Father who keeps on giving,
all because of His gracious love.

So if you do not know Him,
but want to love Him like I do,
it all starts with the choice you make,
for He wants to live in you, too!

I Sing

For I sing
because I'm happy.
I sing because I'm free.
I sing because my Savior,
on Calvary did die for me.

I sing as a way to praise Him.
I sing with prayers lifted above.
I sing to my Heavenly Father,
a song of gratitude and love.

I sing as a messenger for Him,
a song that others may hear.
I sing to the many that are lost
and live in constant fear.

The song I sing is always about Him,
it flows from His Spirit within.
If you listen with your heart, my friends,
it is not me singing, but Him!

A Sinner Knocked On Heavens Door

A sinner knocked on Heavens door,
Jesus met him at the Pearly Gate.
Jesus said to the sinner, "Please come in,
we don't want anyone to have to wait."

So as Jesus was showing the sinner around,
the sinner's eyes was taking everything in.
"How can someone stay in this place?", he asked Jesus,
"how can you want me with all my sin?"

Jesus took the sinner's hand in His,
a smile was on Jesus' face.
He said, "Your sin was all forgiven on the cross,
Heaven has always been your place."

The sinner started singing,
and praising Jesus with a very loud voice.
Then stopped and said, "What about all the others?"
Jesus smiled and said, "It's up to them,
it's their choice!"

Teach Me

Teach me your heart, Lord,
that mine will be changed.
Teach me Your Will, Lord,
so I know how to live each day.

Teach me your love, Lord,
so that with others I might share.
Teach me Your compassion, Lord,
so I may understand how to care.

Teach me Your Word, Lord,
that I may know how to speak.
Teach me Your, paths Lord,
that I may travel with my feet.

Teach me, Lord, please teach me,
for I am nothing without You.
Teach me, Lord, teach me,
before my time on earth is through.

An Empty Container

I am just an empty container,
thirsty to be filled with His love.
I find what He gives me
flows like water from the Heavens above.

Before I yearned to be filled,
I had to yield to His call,
for I was too much into this world,
always stumbling and ready for a fall.

But now that He is within me,
He is satisfying my every need.
All the love He gives me,
I freely pour out to others indeed.

Yes, I am just an empty container,
constantly looking up above,
knowing He will always fill me,
all because of His special love.

For God Is Always There

As you begin your day today,
there is something you must be aware.
You are not traveling through it by yourself,
for God is always there.

Whatever problems come your way,
and they become more than you can bear,
remember not to face them alone,
for God is always there.

When sin is all around you,
to choose it you mustn't dare.
Just focus on Jesus above,
for God is always there.

And when your day is finally done,
give thanks to Him in prayer.
It doesn't matter where you are,
for God is always there.

In Him

In Him I am alive.
In Him I am set free.
Because in Him my friends,
is where I want to be.

In Him life is so abundant.
In Him no cares will there be.
In Him I'll live eternal,
because of His love for me.

In Him the weak are strong.
In Him the blind can see.
In Him the sinners become righteous,
what more could you want, than He?

In Him we are protected.
In Him the demons flee.
In Him I have found myself,
for in Him you'll now find me!

The Church

The church of Christ has many buildings,
some soft, and also some loud.
It is Jesus in the heart of each of us,
that makes us stand out from the crowd.

So pick one where you can praise Him,
make sure from the Bible they do preach,
look to see if the people there,
to the lost, they are looking and trying to reach.

A church is just a building
that people come to seek Him out,
and share His love with others,
yes, that's what church is all about!

So don't get all caught up in the building,
or the name that is attached.
Get caught up in Jesus Christ,
for that is the only church that will last!

People Like You And Me

God looked down from Heaven and said,
"Which ones shall I choose,
to share My Son, Jesus, with,
so no one will have to lose?"

God didn't look for someone perfect,
for on earth no one could be found.
He didn't look for the strongest or the smartest,
so God kept on looking all around.

What God was truly looking for,
was someone who just loved His Son,
someone who believed in the Gospel message,
and the truth it brought to each and everyone.

So God decided to check each heart,
for in there, Jesus' love would truly be.
These were the ones who would share Jesus,
people just like you, Apostle Paul, and people like me.

Your Soul Belongs To Him

As you travel through your day,
though sad or with a grin,
always remember that the soul you carry,
will always belong to Him.

It was created when you were
for a journey that will never end.
Though your body will age and crumble,
your soul does not, my friend.

God's purpose for your soul is simple,
to once again return to Him,
but you have to make the choice,
to be an enemy or be a friend.

So please don't wait another minute,
your soul is what's at stake.
If you don't choose in God,
then it's all for the devil to take!

Our Daily Battles

The battle line was drawn today,
our banner is His cross!
We fight for the many
that are weary and are lost.

The enemy will not give up,
without a lengthy fight.
Fight on, fight on, Christian soldiers,
for our Father gives us the right!

Sing His praises into battle today,
His Word is our mighty sword.
Defeat the many enemies,
repeating what's in His Word!

Fight on through the day,
fight on throughout the night.
Win one more for Jesus,
Heaven is now in sight!

I Can't Do It Alone

I can't do it alone, I said,
was my cry to Heaven above.
The presence of God touched my heart,
giving me strength through His love.

He said, "The fear that you are feeling,
is from your worldly eyes.
Keep them focused on Me, My child,
and My Kingdom will be your prize.

Fill your mind with my Word,
then process it into your heart.
This will always remind you,
we will never be far apart.

Seek out other Christians,
and to My Son Jesus stay so true.
You don't have to do it alone,
We are all here with you."

You Can Have What I Have

You can have what I have,
it is as simple as can be.
This life was meant to be abundant,
and that only comes from Christ, you see.

No matter how hard you try
to live life on your own,
until you live in Him,
loneliness will be your home.

Everything is waiting for you,
it has been there from the start.
All it takes is for you to believe
and ask Jesus into your heart.

Does this make your problems leave?
No, sometimes they may be more,
but what you must understand,
He went through all this before.

So how you decide to live
is completely up to you.
For me, I live for the Son,
see, no other way will do!

I Really Need You Now, Lord

I really need You now, Lord,
yes, please, more and more.
I need to feel Your presence,
now more than ever before.

My heart is becoming empty,
that once was oh so full.
I really need You now Lord,
please touch me if You will.

My heart cries out for peace, Lord,
the peace that only You can give.
I need to rest in You Lord,
it's the only way I can live.

Thank You, my loving Savior,
for always hearing my earthly cries.
I really need You now, Lord,
for without You, how will I ever get by?

Victory Through Jesus

If you battle daily
in this world of sin,
give the fight to Jesus, my friends,
for it's the only way you can win.

If the devil comes upon you,
and there appears no way out,
look to Jesus, my friends,
for that's truly what it's all about.

When bitterness stays with you,
and anger grows within,
release it to Jesus, my friends,
so peace can once again begin.

He can turn dark to light.
He can turn hate to love.
Victory is not in our hands,
but in Christ's hands above.

Hear My Prayer, Lord

So many people in this world
are fighting it every day,
a disease called "cancer",
that tries to take their life away.

It weakens the body,
it plays havoc in their mind,
it doesn't matter who it strikes,
man, woman or child of any kind.

So please hear my prayer, Lord,
may You help us find a way,
to give strength and courage
to those fighting this enemy today.

Give the doctors the wisdom,
to choose what is best,
and also give our researchers,
the funds and knowledge to put it to rest.

Please touch each one afflicted,
and give them peace within their hearts,
let them know You are with them, Lord,
as You have been from the start.

In Jesus precious name,
Amen

A Child Of God

I am a child of Grace,
set free from worldly sin.
I am a child of Righteousness,
because my Savior lives within.

I am a child of Holy Love,
Christ paid the mighty cost.
I am a child of Purity,
my imperfections were nailed to the cross.

I am a child of Eternity,
a life that was created just for Him.
I am His Special child now,
no longer a child to sin.

I am a child of the Master,
in His light is where I trod.
I cry out with a joyful voice,
I am a child of God!!!

God Did Not Leave Us Alone

As we look out our darken windows,
we see the sunshine on our neighbor's home.
Our house is filled with misery,
but our God did not leave us alone.

As we looked for ways to make ends meet,
and see so many over flowing pockets shown,
oh where will our next meal come from?
But our God did not leave us alone.

As we see the many healthy people,
yet our bodies ache and groan,
we cannot go from here to there,
but our God did not leave us alone.

See it doesn't matter what we are going through,
but with the Lord how much we have grown.
It is not about what others have and we don't,
but that our God did not leave us alone.

What Makes It Great

There is a beginning
and there is an end.
There are enemies
and there are friends.

There is love
and there is hate.
There is average,
then there is great.

There are winners,
and there are losers too.
There are non-believers,
but I believe in You!

For Jesus is the beginning
and also my best Friend,
because of His love for me,
there never will be an end.

See, we are what we choose,
I chose love over hate.
I am a winner through Christ Jesus,
Him living in me, is what makes it great!

God's Measuring Stick

God called me to His throne of Grace,
and said, "Let's see if you measure up!"
An angel brought His measuring stick,
the Fruits of the Spirit marked bottom to top.

So as I stood next to His measuring stick,
I passed the love, joy and peace.
He smiled and then said, "Child of Mine,
these are so very important to Me."

Next came long-suffering, then
kindness, goodness and faith.
I also passed each one of those,
God nodded His approval but then said, "Wait."

I saw you were arguing with
a Brother and Sister from church.
You didn't appear to be in control,
you appeared angry and very hurt.

With down cast eyes I said,
"Forgive me Father, for it is true,
the reason that it happened
was I took my eyes off of You!

Choose Or Lose

With each day that comes anew,
with it comes new challenges too.
Some are little but some are great,
those are the ones where your heart will break.

We try our best each day to get through,
but those heartbreakers are tough for me and you.
But in the Bible if you do read,
Jesus said, "Give them all to me!"

It is not just the great challenges that He does care,
but everything in our life He wants to share.
See, our heartaches, our joys, our tears and smiles,
He wants to be a part of them forever, not just awhile.

So it's up to us as to what we choose,
without Christ in our lives, we surely will lose.
In happiness or in sorrow, what comes our way,
the praise goes to God, for loving us each day!

The Way Out

I was lost and confused,
I wandered about,
then I heard through His Word,
"I Am the Way out."

From my eyes I couldn't see
where I was to go,
He spoke to my heart,
"Let Me show you, I love you so!"

What seemed all dark,
from His Word became light,
He took all my wrongs,
and made me all right!

I said, "Lord, please tell me.
what for You can I do?"
He answered, "My Child,
tell others, for they need to know too!"

Why Do I Love Him

Why do I love Him,
well, it's plain to see,
even though it was over 2000 years ago,
Jesus died on the cross for me.

Why did He do it?
Why did He suffer all that pain?
It was all because of love,
and I know He would do it again!

See, He knew me before I knew Him,
He claimed me for His own.
He wants me to spend eternity with Him,
together in His heavenly home.

All I had to do was choose
to accept His act of love.
I hope you choose as I did,
so we all can be together above.

The Mission

I was called by the Almighty,
for He had a mission for me.
He said, "I need for you to touch the hearts
of the many people that still can't see.

I want you to share My love,
and reassure them My Word is true.
Tell them in whatever way you can,
in the best way that you can do.

Tell them through My poems,
show them through your love,
sing to them in hymns and songs,
that I am in control from above.

Tell them they don't have to worry,
for with Me there is nothing to hide.
Tell them time is getting short,
the great I Am is waiting for them to decide!"

God's Timing

God's timing is so awesome,
though sometimes we just don't see,
He is always working in our lives,
guiding us in what's good for you and me.

It seems we only see Him working,
when so much trouble comes our way,
but God is still working in the good days,
to make sure life always stays that way.

But we are an anxious people,
we want everything now for we can't wait.
We always fail to remember,
God's always on time and never late.

His timing is not our timing,
His ways are always right.
Please remember to thank Him,
before you go to sleep tonight.

What Are You Choosing

Which way are you going today?
Will you make a turn or will you go straight?
Life is filled with questions,
it is all up to us the choice we make.

Will you try to help someone else today,
or will you just look out for yourself?
Will you pursue the purpose God has for you,
or just keep running all in doubt?

Will you stop and look at all the blessings,
into your life you do receive?
Or will you think you did it all yourself,
is this what you truly believe?

Well, whatever you choose it is up to you,
but remember there are consequences at stake.
See, it is not about this life but the next,
and the choices through life we make.

For me, I choose to follow Christ,
to Him my life I did freely give.
He is making the decisions for me,
yep, that's my choice how to live!

The Many Parts Of Faith

Faith has many parts,
all are needed to endure.
See, "All things are possible
if you believe", that's for sure.

For the way of faith is not easy,
it takes trials, discipline, courage and more.
For if we walk by faith and not by sight,
that is God's way to make us soar.

We must keep on believing in His Word.
Don't be moved away by what you feel or see.
For the victory of faith is in God's timing,
our part is to stay steady, you and me.

So remember to stay unmoved,
use your discipline of faith to stay so true.
Every petition we put before the Lord,
we should say, "Now Lord, we are waiting on You!"

How Can This Still Be

God loves me, oh so much,
in a very special way.
He wants only the best for me,
as He is with me every day.

He watches over me
every morning, noon and night.
He corrects me when I'm wrong,
always remaining special in His sight.

God directs my feet only in
the paths that pleases Him.
He opens doors to the lost,
then encourages me to enter in.

He speaks to my heart through scripture,
then says, "Tell others of Me."
I am still amazed many still don't know Him,
can someone tell me, how can this still be?

The Victory

The enemy is all around us
and Cancer is its name.
It robs our joy, steals our strength
and crushes families along the way.

It doesn't matter who it attacks,
youth, middle age or the aged.
Its mission is to destroy,
for it knows no other way.

But I know of One who is stronger,
who has overcome each battle, and has won.
So put your life in Jesus hands, my friends,
He's been winning since time has begun.

Cancer's days are numbered,
like all our enemies that we face.
In Christ there is always victory,
given to us because of His grace.

The victory is here on earth,
and guaranteed in Heaven above.
The final battle was won on the cross,
Jesus proved it through His love.

Choose Wisely ✓

There is a right way of doing things,
there is also a wrong way too.
Whichever you decide to do,
most times determines what happens to you.

You can decide to live on junk food,
then pay a lot in doctor bills, is what you'll do.
Or you can choose the food that's healthy,
see, it is all what you decide to choose.

You can choose to live a sinful life,
but then in hell eternity you will spend.
Or you can choose a life with Christ,
where joy, peace, happiness and love will never end.

There are not a lot of decisions,
that the good Lord will have us make,
It is either right or wrong,
but remember what you choose
will determine your fate!

Within An Instant

My heart was broke, I cried to the Lord,
"Please help me Lord, what can I do?"
Within an instant I heard His voice,
"I am here My child, I will mend it for you!"

I was lost and confused, I cried to the Lord,
"Please help me Lord, I really lost my way."
Within an instant I heard His voice,
"Give Me your hand, I will guide you today!"

I was all alone, I cried to the Lord,
"Please help me Lord, no one seems to care."
Within an instant I felt His presence,
His love was everywhere.

Within an instant whenever I cried,
the Lord was always there for me.
He wants to be there for you too,
if only you will open your heart to see.

Tell Them For Me

He wants to bless you in a special way,
so He asked me to let you know that today.
He said, "Tell them I have all they need,
all they have to do is trust and believe."

He said, "Tell them not to worry and fall prey,
to what they see and hear in the world these days."
Then He said, "Tell them in a way they can hear,
tell them My love and grace is nothing to fear!

Tell them from My Word they must read,
it is important for them to understand and take heed.
Tell them through My poetry and through My songs,
write it and sing it so they understand they belong.

Tell them, tell them, that they must make a choice,
tell them for Me, for you are My voice.
Tell them all, to not listen would be a mistake,
tell them My child before it's too late."

The Treasures Of Heaven

The treasures of Heaven are waiting for you,
they are all ready for you to claim.
Each one of us must first believe,
then receive them in Jesus name.

But to me what is most interesting,
as I travel along life's way,
I need not wait to enter into Heaven,
for I can claim my treasures today.

Heaven's treasures are for earth too,
like good health, family and friends.
We do not have to wait to receive them,
receive them now not just at your journey's end.

So thank You, Heavenly Father,
for these treasures you have for me.
I pray all would realize it too,
for in Your Word it states, "if only we believe."

What Can I Do For You

What do you want me to do today, Lord?
What can I do for You?
Direct my path where You want me to walk.
Open my eyes that I may see You there too.

What do You want me to say today, Lord?
Please give me the Words to speak.
Open my ears to the lost in this world.
May they hear the cries of the weak.

What do You want me to do today, Lord?
How may I serve You today?
Please touch my heart with Your love,
so I can share it in Your special way.

What can I do for You, Lord?
Each day You do everything for me.
How can I serve You better?
Lord, please tell me, what can it be?

At The Feet Of Jesus

At the feet of Jesus
is where I want to be.
Leaving all of my old self
renewed in His victory.

At the feet of Jesus,
I will surrender it all to Him.
I will hold nothing back,
for that is where my new life begins.

At the feet of Jesus,
I come in awe and song.
I bow before my loving God,
yes, this is where I truly belong.

At the feet of Jesus,
thank You Father, for Your Son.
It's sweet to sing His praises,
as each day on earth moves along.

A Hug

A hug is a special gift
sent from God above.
He touches some ones heart and says,
"Hug that person with my love."

He uses different people,
to accomplish this task for Him.
It could be a family member,
or a lot of times, just a friend.

But what the hug symbolizes
is Him reaching down from above.
He tells the one doing the hugging,
squeeze them for me with all you got.

The hug means you are special,
and may help to make your day.
To God it means I love you,
in a very, very special way!

So if someone wants to hug you,
for they think you may need a lift,
remember it is God doing the hugging,
please accept this, it's His special gift.

I Need To Talk, Lord

I need to talk, Lord,
for I have a lot on my mind.
I am worried for some friends,
battling sicknesses of various kinds.

I also have friends
that are living all alone.
Many have also lost a lot of things,
like family, jobs and homes.

Please help me understand, Lord,
why all this has to be.
See Lord, when my family and friends hurt,
it is just like it is happening to me.

Tell me Lord, what can I do,
to help them through these days?
Direct me to Your Word, Lord,
so I can share with them what it says.

Thank You again, Lord,
for listening to me once again.
I am so blessed You always take the time,
and blessed because You are my Friend!

Wit's End

When you are at your wits end,
you will find that God lives there.
He is always waiting for our problems,
to show us how much He cares.

He is with us through the good times,
but the bad ones is where He shines.
He's waiting for our cries of help,
He is listening all the time.

So when you are at your wits end,
and you don't know what to do,
remember that is where you'll find God,
for He is waiting to hear from you.

He will take your hardest problem,
and make it turn out right.
He is always working at wit's end,
every morning, noon and night!

What Would Jesus Do

WWJD is a question,
that has been said many times.
When you ask yourself this question,
your life will stay in line.

In line with creation,
the way life was meant to be,
Keep asking WWJD,
and believe me you will see.

WWJD is a daily guide,
to guide you on your way,
for there isn't a better role model,
than Jesus, to follow day by day.

What would Jesus do?
Just grab your Bible and read.
He answers all the questions for us,
all we have to do is believe!

The Hurting, The Lost, And The Cross

There are many people that are hurting,
and many that are lost and don't know the Way.
My prayer is that as they read this poem,
it may lead them to Jesus today.

When we celebrate Christmas,
it is a special time of year.
We sing praises to the Christ Child,
who was born into this world of fear.

No one had a room for Him,
many just turned them away.
Would it have made a difference knowing,
on the Cross He would die for us one day?

Just stop for a moment and think of this,
what if it all happened just today?
Would you have let the Christ Child in?
Would you have room for Him today?

Nothing really has changed,
in the 2000 plus years.
See, we still are all hurting and lost,
living in this world of fear.

We can't have the baby,
without having the Cross,
and we wouldn't have had either one,
if not for the hurting and the lost!

Having A Bad Day

So you are having a bad day,
you shouldn't feel alone.
So many others are having one too,
in this temporary world we call home.

It is not about the struggle,
or even the pain you are going through.
It is what you can learn and do through it,
and knowing God is there for you.

It is not about the "Why me, Lord?"
Think of the Apostle Paul if you do.
See, He understood and walked closely with God,
no matter what he was going through.

In this life we are going to have problems,
that translates to many bad days.
Grasp on tightly to the good ones,
and because of them, give God all the praise!

This Side Of Heaven

I woke up this morning
on this side of Heaven,
I said, "Good morning, Lord,
thank You for this day I was given!"

Then I said, "I love You, Lord,
what can I do for You?
Please guide me to the lost,
so I can share You with them too!"

On this side of Heaven,
there is so much to do.
Day by day helping others,
in whatever they need to get through.

See, on this side of Heaven,
there will always be need.
It is our job, as Children of God,
to show Christ in whatever it be.

One day will surely come,
when our work will finally be done,
and we will leave this side of Heaven,
to be with the Father and His glorious Son!

Jesus Winked

I was at a nursing home today,
where I go to give God's love.
Many, many people living there,
all in desperate need of His special touch.

So after I sang my heart out,
and because of Him all were blessed,
I started to visit one by one,
saying God loves them and to all the rest.

Then I came to a gentleman,
his body could not move.
It appeared as though he was stuck,
or to the bed chair he was glued.

I touched him on the shoulder
and then he winked which made me think,
I told him he just made my day,
my friends, I think I just saw Jesus wink!

He Chose Us

The Father was talking with His Son,
"Which one are you going to choose?",
"All of them", Jesus said.
The Father replied, "With some you might lose?"

"Yes, I know, Father", Jesus said,
"but they must decide what to do.
As My love is freely given, must also be freely received,
just like Your love for Me and Mine for You!"

Then the Father said to His Son,
"There will be hurt and there will be pain."
Jesus answered, "Yes, Father I know,
but because of My love for them, it is all for their gain."

So, my friends, please choose wisely,
take some time and consider the loss.
I don't know about you, my friends
but I am glad He chose us!

There Lies Life's Key

I read from a friend,
"He must become greater,
I must become less!"
My friends, there lies life's key.
See, it is hard for us to understand,
but it is not about you or me.

We all have choices to make,
either they will be good
or they will be very bad,
consequences there surely will be.
If you choose to live His life,
ah, my friends, there lies life's key.

See, ever since He said,
"Let there be light",
it was for Him and Him alone,
light for only Him to see.
But then as He created everything else,
He wanted to share it with you and me.

So get your eyes off yourself,
and look to others so you might help,
as you give praise to the Lord above.
I pray that you can understand like me.
See, everything we do must be for Him,
for there lies life's key.

The Pit

I found myself falling,
deep into a pit.
The more I tried to climb out,
the farther down I would get.

Nothing to grab onto,
the light began to fade.
What would I do,
who could help me here today?

I just felt so helpless,
what is this going to bring?
The pit of despair
is not a wonderful thing.

Help me, help me,
I cried out in vain.
Then all of a sudden,
I remembered His wonderful name.

Jesus said, "Whatever you ask
in My Name, I will give to you."
I cried, "Jesus, please save me now,
I am lost and don't know what to do!"

Then within an instant,
I felt His hand of grace.
He pulled me from the pit
to a wonderful safe place.

So as you read this poem,
and in a pit you might be,
cry out the name of Jesus,
my friends, it worked for me.

Just A Bump In The Road

So many times on this road called "life",
we find the road is not very smooth.
There are just a few bumps in the road,
to try and make us move.

A smooth road is a happy road,
with no troubles along the way.
But what we find is, Jesus said it best,
"You will have trials and tribulations some days!"

These trials could be because of your health,
or maybe because of a lost relationship today.
But for sure it is just a bump in the road,
as you travel on life's road each day.

But what is most important
when you hit a bump like this,
remember Jesus hit it with you,
because if you let Him, you are His!

He will direct you in the path that is right,
and smooth out the road along your way.
See, no matter what bump you hit,
He will get you over it today!

A Broken Heart

A broken heart cannot be healed,
by either you or me.
It must be healed by our Creator,
for He first put it together, you see.

He knows every little part,
that in this life might break.
He knows the pain that goes with it,
for His own heart once did break.

I asked Him, "What can I do,
to mend my heart that did break?"
He said, "Nothing My child,
I will do it for you, definitely time it will take."

So each day that passes,
I know my heart will heal,
and what is truly amazing about it,
is how close to Jesus each day I do feel!

The Flame Of Love

Christ's love starts as a little flame,
then grows into a raging fire.
His love can find you anywhere,
no matter where you were or where you are.

His love is the warmth needed
to cure a cold, callous heart.
He forgives what we've done in the past,
and freely gives us a fresh new start.

Once His flame is in you,
you will never be the same.
To get the flame of love started,
just call out in Jesus name.

Then His Spirit lives within you,
the fuel needed for the fire to rage.
Grab onto His flame of love, my friends,
once you do, you'll never be the same!

Walking Together For Jesus

Walking together for Jesus,
as Christians is what we do.
Do not let any worldly circumstances
distract His walk with you.

With our eyes may we be looking
for wherever there is a need.
May we also be prepared
in others to plant His seed.

Walking together for Jesus,
staying strong in His Word,
always being ready to share it with
the many that haven't heard.

Oh what a path of glory,
that as Christians, by grace we walk.
Oh what a Gospel message,
from His heart He gave us to talk.

Walk with me, Brother's and Sister's,
united in One accord,
walking together for Jesus,
our Savior and our Lord!

Did Anyone See Jesus

"Where is Jesus?"
asked the homeless man on the street.
"Yes, where is He?" the addict echoed,
"Can someone send Him to me?"

"Where is He?",
said a woman, raising her kids alone.
"If He is the God of love,
then why hasn't He come?"

"Where is Jesus?"
asked a man from a prison cell.
"We all need Him now,
can anyone to us please tell?"

"Has anyone seen Jesus?",
asked a business man in a suit.
"My business is going under
and I don't know what to do."

Then they all heard a child
singing, "Jesus loves me this I know."
Everyone looking for Jesus asked,
"Did you see Jesus, tell us where did He go?"

The child just smiled,
and then touched his heart.
"There is Jesus", he said,
"He's been right there from the start!"

So the moral of this poem,
wherever you are, or whatever you need,
the Answer has always been there,
from God's heart, to mine, to yours indeed!

He Lovingly Kissed My Soul

The Lord grabbed onto my heart,
He caressed it and made it whole.
Then He did what no other could do,
He lovingly kissed my soul!

I felt a flame ignite within me,
a heat from love that I had to share.
He kissed my soul in such a way,
I knew just how much He cared.

Not only did He die for me,
alone on a wooden cross,
but He never gave up loving me,
He found me when I was lost.

I am a changed person now,
no longer broken, but now whole.
See, Jesus made my life complete,
as He lovingly kissed my soul!

I Am A Past Sinner

I am a past sinner,
praise God that now I see,
before He came into my life,
the worldly sin was controlling me.

Even though I didn't want it to,
there was nothing stronger to set me free,
but then I heard the Gospel message
that God gave His Son, for me!

So for a moment I stopped and thought,
the God of all Creation did that for me?
How could I then let this worldly sin
keep me from being free?

I raised my head up to the sky
and said, "Jesus, set me free!
Come into my heart today,
I want You, not sin, in me!"

Then within the moment,
through Jesus I became a winner,
my past is just that now,
for because of Him, I am no longer a sinner!

Life's Storms

Another storm is on its way,
Jesus said, "Do not fear today,
for storms will come and storms will leave,
stay firm in Me, this you must believe.

If you feel weak when in the storm,
My strength will keep you from all harm.
When darkness is all that you see,
I'll be your light, please believe in Me.

When in the storm no help you find,
go to MY Word and refresh the mind.
Let it sink deep within your heart,
then you will see the storm depart.

Life's storms are plenty but with them bring
you closer to Me so you can cling.
Hold tight, My child, to MY love so true,
for in each storm, I'll be with you!"

My Crystal Tears

Every time my heart did break
and tears rolled down my face,
Jesus captured each one of them,
and in His heart He did place.

He kept them oh so close to Him,
because He also felt the pain,
He knew there would be more to fall,
because my heart would break again.

But what He did with my tears,
no one else could ever do,
He turned them into crystal jewels,
all because His love, was oh, so true.

So one day when we meet above,
what He collected through all the years,
He will give to me a jeweled crown,
made up from all my crystal tears.

The End Is The Beginning

Death is the gate to life,
one that all must pass through.
The question lies in the journey,
that decision is up to you.

If you think it is all about this life,
well, I'm sorry for I disagree.
My friends, this life is all about learning,
learning about His love for you and me.

See once we have the knowledge,
then we cannot say we did not know.
All that remains is our choice
to where our souls will go.

So choose wisely what you decide,
and in this life what you do.
See, the end is really the beginning,
of what becomes of me and you.

So I have made my decision,
I pray yours will be the same.
My soul is headed for Heaven,
I can say this in Jesus name.

We Are All The Same

One day I asked the Lord,
"Why am I so different when people look at me?"
He said, "Let me turn everyone inside out,
then tell Me what you see!"

I said, "We are all the same,
Lord, how can that be?
How can the outside be so different,
oh if only people could see.

It is not how we look,
but what we say and do.
It is not that our outsides are different,
but about the love that shines through.

It is not about where we are
or really from where we came.
For we were created in Your image,
praise to You, we are all the same!"

See This Love Within Me

See this love within me,
as it grows from day to day.
A love that burned for me also,
from Calvary's hill so far away.

See this love within me,
so pure and oh so free,
a love that made my Savior cry,
"Father don't blame them, blame Me!"

Hear His love flow from my lips,
as I share for all to hear.
See this love within me,
may it touch all those that are near.

His love grows even stronger
with each breath that I take.
May you feel this love also,
please don't make our Savior wait!

Touch A Life

Touch a life within this day,
show someone you care today.

Make a difference by what you do,
reach out in love, as Christ reached out to you.

Look all around where there is need,
touch a life for Jesus indeed.

Share His love that others might know,
He loves us all, yes He loves us so.

So wherever you go or whatever you do,
touch a life for God, He wants you to.

Someone is waiting, to feel His love,
It is not you touching them, but the Father above!

Walking This Lonely Land

As I walk this lonely land,
I am waiting to go home.
For where my feet are walking,
I feel lonely and all alone.

My heart is in another place,
where I have yet to be,
and deep within this heart of mine,
Jesus is calling to me.

All that stands between us
is time and His work to be done.
Heaven is my real home,
where Jesus waits for everyone.

But not all will go there,
because they won't truly believe.
They put their trust in this earthly place,
well, my friends, not me!

I made my choice and
I gave my all to Him.
One day, yes one sweet day,
He will say, "Child of Mine, come on in!"

Is There Something I Can Do

What can I do or what can I say,
is there something from me
that will bring you to Jesus today?

If you know Him but a little and want more,
is there something I can do for you,
for like an eagle to make His presence soar?

How can I show you and make you see,
Holy Spirit please give me the words,
touch their hearts, release them, make them free.

Open my eyes and reveal through the Word,
give me the boldness to speak Your message,
please open their ears so it can be heard.

Oh Precious Father who reigns up above,
please tell me what I can do and what can I say,
it is so important for all, to feel Your love!

The Heart Of Christ

The heart of Christ,
may it beat in me.
May each ounce of His blood
continue to keep me free.

May His compassion for all,
in me forever burn.
May His love for every person,
be what my own heart yearns.

The heart of my Savior,
so strong and so true.
May it flow from my lips,
from His heart, to mine, to you.

The heart of Christ,
may each person find.
For it replenishes the soul,
and gives peace to the mind.

The heart of Christ,
His love from day one,
there for all to partake,
since each life has begun!

Broken And Wounded

So many people
in need today.
So many lives
just being wasted away.

So many are broken
and wounded they stay.
All are looking for someone
to show them the Way.

They fear of the preachers
and the words that they say.
Their hearts cannot receive
the Gospel message today.

Remember, my fellow Christians,
it is important what we do,
to show to the unbelievers,
we were once broken and wounded too.

Please keep sharing the message
and show what Christ does for you.
Pray to the Lord up above,
that the message will get through.

Do You Have Time For Him

Do you have time for Him?
He always has time for you.
Are you willing to share your life with Him?
That is what He is waiting for you to do!

Are you spending every minute,
living in this world of sin?
Do you have any time, my friends?
Do you have any time for Him?

Everything you are looking for
and everything that you already have,
is from the Lord above and no one else,
aren't you glad He took His time and always has?

Do you have time for Him?
If not I suggest you do.
He is waiting on you, my friends,
take some time for Him, he's waiting for you!

Speak To Them For Me

The Lord touched my heart and said,
"You heard my voice because of your love,
so speak to them for Me,
tell them what I am saying from above.

Tell them from My Word
and through poems and songs.
Speak to them for Me,
each day as you go along.

To those that will listen,
My love will shine through.
Speak to them for Me,
this is what I am asking of you.

Give words of encouragement
to those that are in need,
one day all will hear Me as you do,
if only they will truly believe!"

Then, within the moment
I knew what I had to do,
Keep speaking His words of love
before my life was through.

I hear Him because I want to,
that is why it is plain to see.
I will obey what He asked,
when He said, "Speak to them for Me!"

Man Of God

He is a very quiet man,
not many know he is there.
But one thing they all understand,
he loves praying for them in his prayers.

He doesn't have a lot of family,
friends are just a few.
But this quiet man knows God
and he talks to Him, about you and others too.

He smiles at all he would meet
and he will say, "God bless and I love you!'
A quiet man of a few words,
but a man of God, through and through.

Oh, he isn't perfect
and he never claims to be.
He never is embarrassed to say,
"See, how Jesus has changed me?"

So one day will surely come,
when he will be called away.
For this man of God, his job will be done,
no more reason for him to stay.

So if you happen to meet him,
there is something special that you will see.
It is God working through him,
like He wants to do for you and me.

This Message Is For You

God spoke to my heart and said,
"Tell them for Me that my love is true.
Ask them, what more can I say,
or what more can I do?

I gave you everything,
My only Son, so you would see.
What more can I give?
His sacrifice was for you, not for Me.

The air that you breathe,
I created for you.
The water you drink,
I gave you that too!

The food that you eat,
the clothes on your back,
I made sure you have everything,
because of My love, you would never lack."

Then God's voice was silent,
what He was saying had to be through.
So, my friends, all I can add is,
"This message is for you!"

Broken Heart, Healed Heart

I brought my broken heart to the Father
and said, "Please, fix for me!"
He looked down from the throne and said,
"My child, Mine was broken and nailed to a tree!

I know the pain and how it feels,
I know it seems it will never end,
but I made hearts to be broken,
so they could be made stronger and mend again.

See, MY Son's heart was broken,
because so many just wouldn't believe.
You cannot live in this sinful world
and have your heart always remain free.

So if your heart becomes broken,
how you heal it, is with love.
From family, friends and sharing it with others,
until we all can be together above!"

Winning Through My Sufferings

I am winning through my sufferings,
rejoicing through my pains.
Singing praises to my Savior,
through my tears that fall like rain.

It matters not of my trials,
for He has suffered before me.
I am winning through my sufferings,
I pray that the entire world can see.

Suffering is a part of life,
that no one can escape.
The question is what you do through it,
for this is what makes life great.

Take your eyes off yourself,
watch for other people's pain.
That is when you truly win
and though suffering, you will gain.

See, everyone is having problems,
in this life they will never end.
So I give mine to Jesus,
that is why He is my best Friend!

Meet Me At The Cross

I heard a voice in my heart,
it was Jesus and He said to me,
"Meet Me at the Cross,
tell others so they can also see.

Calvary is not that far away,
like Me, it should be in your heart.
Meet Me at the Cross,
for that is where life truly starts.

Don't get caught up in this world,
for it will soon be gone away.
It is just temporary for all,
not a place to always stay.

Meet Me at the Cross,
it is there we become One,
I will be waiting for you,
Please, will you take the time to come?"

I Came Back To The Cross Today

I came back to the cross today,
for there I had to be.
I brought all my cares and pains
and left them there at His feet.

I knelt there for a while,
for close to Him I wanted to be.
I came back to the cross today,
I left my heart there at Calvary.

My pain became His pain,
my sorrows He took them all.
I came back to the cross today
and this is what I saw.

I saw my love nailed to it,
I saw all my guilt and shame,
I saw the Son of Man looking down at me
and then He said my name.

His cross is forever with me now,
and this is what I know.
I picked up my cross and followed Him,
for my life is His and not my own.

So if you are ever in doubt
and it appears you lost your way,
return to the cross, my friends,
He is waiting for you today!

Each Day Is Different

Each day is different,
like a snowflake, not one the same.
If one day it had sunshine,
the next may have rain.

If one day it is hot,
the next could be very cold.
Each day is different,
something to truly behold.

But in each one the same always is true,
no matter what ever will change.
God's love will never
and many people still find that strange.

Strange because everything else changes,
but not His love for you and me.
Oh, each day is different, my friends,
but praise God, not Him, you see.

So don't try to change Him,
for that can never be,
what has to change is us,
like each day, you and me.

Change from our sinful life,
to a life glorified in Him.
For if we do not change,
in Heaven we could never enter in!

He Touched My Soul

I never thought that anyone
could ever make me whole,
then I felt His divine presence
and He touched my soul.

He changed my life completely
in ways you may never know,
all because of His love for me,
He touched my soul.

He filled what was missing,
He mended what was broke,
He reached within my inner being
and touched my soul with one stroke.

Now I am complete,
no longer a part but a whole,
my life really began the moment
He touched my soul!

He Is Waiting For You

Another day will come
and then it will pass
and still so many,
will miss His grasp.

Our hearts were made
to yearn for Him.
Yet for so many they question,
where do I begin?

The answer is simple
and is for all to see.
All you do is ask,
"Lord, please come to me!"

Wherever you are,
whatever you do,
God the Father,
is waiting for you.

Today Is Sunday

Today is Sunday,
I am off to go see Him.
I will read from His Word
and praise Him as I sing.

I will fellowship with others,
most that believe as I do.
Some may be there just to see,
if what the Bible teaches is true.

Today is Sunday,
just one day out of the week.
But this day is so important,
for it brings hope and strength for the weak.

Thank You Lord,
for this day that is all about You.
But what many don't understand,
the other six days should also be too!

To And Fro

I looked for You,
I cried, "Where can You be?
Lord, how can I go on?
please Lord, come to me!

The peace that I need,
You can only give,
without You Lord,
I don't know how to live."

I searched to and fro,
and then I just stood still.
My heart became peaceful,
as I listened for His will.

Then within the moment,
everything was made all right.
I realized You didn't leave me,
for the moment I just lost sight.

We don't have to look to and fro,
for it is written You will never leave.
All we have to do is rest in You
and to do that we must truly believe!

Get Behind Me Satan

Get behind me Satan,
for that is where you must be.
May my eyes ever be cast forward,
for Jesus, is what I want to see.

May my ears be listening to the Spirit,
so they do not hear your lies.
Get behind me Satan,
may this be my daily cry.

Stay away from my family
and all my friends too.
Get behind them Satan,
their lives do not belong to you.

Your time is almost over,
praise God it will surely end.
So stay behind me Satan,
that's where you belong until then!

Some Say ✓

Some say, "I am foolish because for others I do care."
Some say, "They don't understand
why I take my time to share."
Some say, "How can he love a God he cannot see?"
Jesus said, "Tell them it's all because of Me!"

Some say, "I spend too much time
helping in God's church."
Some say, "Why is he always trying
to help the ones that hurt?"
Some say, "Why does he do that, what can it be?"
Jesus said, "Tell them it's all because of Me!"

Some say, "I am wasting all my time,
telling others about Him."
Some say, "It's impossible to be born again!"
Some say, "Why from the Bible does he read?"
Jesus said, "Tell them it's all because of Me!"

Some say, "Why does he pray
for those he does not know?"
Some say, "Is it possible he does love them so?"
Some say, "Why is he so happy and seem so free?'
Jesus said, "Tell them it's all because of Me!"

Why The Smile

Why the smile, someone asked,
when you should really be sad.
How can you smile through all this,
please tell me if you can.

How can you smile
with so many problems ahead,
most would want to give up
and probably wish they were dead.

Well, I said,
with a very large grin,
it's because of Jesus,
because of Him, I know I win!

See, problems will come
and then they will leave.
But not Jesus' love,
this you must believe.

So learn from this life
and as you go through it smile.
The reason being, this one
only lasts for a little while.

Now grab on to Jesus
and be glad you had.
For eternity with Him,
you never will be sad!

See, when we enter Heaven,
that's when true happiness begins.
I hope that answers the question,
why I always grin!

The Gift

Thank You for Your gift to me,
the gift of love nailed to that tree.
Thank You for Your sacrifice,
You gave Your life,
so mine could be made right.

What a gift that was given,
sent from the Father above.
It wasn't that I was worthy of it,
no, given just because of love.

How amazing when I think,
that no other gift can compare,
and when one receives it,
with others we want to share.

May each day I walk this earth,
Your gift of love I share.
For now I finally realize,
my purpose for being here.

Nothing More

There is only one way to love Him.
There is only one thing you must do.
You must open up your heart and say,
"Jesus, my heart belongs to You!"

There is no one who loves you more,
not one with a love like His.
So open up your heart
and to Jesus freely give.

Give because you want to.
Give because He gave to you.
Your heart truly belongs to Him,
all you have to do is choose.

Each minute you wait is costly,
for the previous one could be your last.
What is important to Jesus is the present,
see, He has forgiven what you did in the past.

So decide now to give Him
what He is waiting for,
your decision to love Him,
that's all He wants, nothing more!

Wait On Him

I was in the midst of my problems,
I prayed to God but an answer did not see,
I asked the Lord, "Why?"
He replied, "You did not wait for Me!"

I cried out, "I love You Lord!
I need You now, right away!
Then He spoke to me again
and said, "Please listen to what I say.

It's not about the problem,
or what you are going through,
it is what we will do together,
see, it is not just about you.

So, don't look at your problems,
stay strong, wait for Me, and rest.
The key is always waiting on Me,
for I truly know what's best.

So while you are waiting for Me,
look around, for others have problems too.
Maybe they don't know Me like you do,
so you could help them to get through!"

A Love Just For Me

Every now and then,
a special love happens by.
It stays for just a short time,
then leaves, why I know not why.

One such a love
did happen to come my way.
It grabbed onto my heart
and with me will always stay.

The presence of true love,
when bonded remains strong.
Nothing can take it away
when in this life things do go wrong.

Praise God for the memories
and for the ability to always see,
He gave me such a special gift,
a love just for me!

Jesus Is The Light

Today it's sunny outside,
but for many it is dark as can be.
For in this sinful world
no light can they see.

The darkness is the tsunami,
that washed their life into the sea.
To some the darkness is an addiction,
that will not let them live to be free.

A relationship gone forever
is dark as dark can be.
The homeless people living in the streets
in the dark cry out, "What about me?"

And through all this darkness,
there is a light that will not fade.
In the scriptures it is written,
Jesus is the light and the only way.

So wherever your darkness is,
for in this sinful life there will definitely be,
open your heart to Jesus, my friends,
for He has removed the darkness for me!

It Doesn't Matter Lord

It doesn't matter, Lord,
what will come my way.
For I know You are in me
and we are One this day.

It doesn't matter, Lord,
living in this world of sin,
because of Your love,
the outcome is, I win!

It doesn't matter, Lord,
the trials and tribulations on me,
what matters Lord, is You!
I am so blessed, this is what I see.

I see only You, Lord,
and I pray that will always be.
May everything I do, Lord,
prove You are what really matters to me!

His Fire Within

There is a raging fire,
that within me always burns.
It is for the love of Christ,
that my heart increasingly yearns.

This fire keeps getting stronger
with each and every passing day.
It makes me cry out to the lost,
"Christ is the only way!"

It puts me on my knees,
for I know I am not my own.
For I was purchased with a price
and promised a heavenly home.

Lord, please hear my cry,
"Never let this fire die out!
My life is always Yours,
that's what this life is all about!"

The Love Of Jesus

I do not need to be great,
I do not want fame.
All I need is the love of Jesus,
that I claim in His Holy Name.

I do not need to be wealthy,
I do not need all the possessions it brings.
It is the love of Jesus
that makes my heart to sing.

I do not need knowledge,
so I can be smarter than all the rest.
What I need is His Holy Word
that guides me through each of life's tests.

I do not need recognition
from all my family and friends.
All I need is the love of Jesus
that will endure and has no end.

So what do you need?
What is it that gets you through the day?
For me, it's the love of Jesus,
and that's all I have to say!

A God's Day Is Upon Us

A God's day is upon us
to do His work for Him.
We can accomplish nothing for Him,
if by ourselves we let the day begin.

There is so much to do,
so many people that we must see.
So many hearts still in bondage,
that God wants to be free.

But we cannot do this
by our own power and ways.
We need to rest in the Lord
and listen to what He says.

His Word is our daily guide,
that through it, we will not fail.
It contains His Gospel message of love,
that as Children of His we must go and tell.

So don't let this day slip by,
for there is so much we must do.
Look out to help others, not yourself,
for God will take care of you!

Is Just A Mere Bag Of Shells

This life isn't about money,
or what you have in the end.
It's about being honest with yourself
and being able to call someone a friend.

This life isn't about status,
or who you may crush on the way up.
It's about thinking and giving to others,
instead of grabbing everything for yourself.

This life isn't about envy,
or wishing what someone has, you had.
It's about being thankful to God above,
for what He gave you, and then being glad.

Nope, this life is not about money, envy, or status,
it's about love and in your heart what it tells.
See, everything else when it comes down to it
is just a mere bag of shells!

The Robe Of Righteousness

I was called to the throne room,
where God wanted to give something to me,
it was the robe of righteousness,
white as white can be.

I said, "Father how can that be mine,
for all the sins in the past?"
The Father of Creation smiled and said,
"They are forgiven, which means they cannot last!"

Then in the room came Jesus,
He took His robe and gave it to me.
He smiled and said, "This is yours now,
I was saving it for you until that day you would believe!

See, the black marks of sin are gone,
only the purity of white remains.
You can wear the robe of righteous now,
all because you truly believe in My name.

Your sins are no longer part of you,
for you are now totally free.
Your sins were left on the cross,
covered by My blood at Calvary!"

One Day Soon

One day soon, all the non-believers
will find out it was true.
One day soon, sweet Jesus,
they will all agree, it is about You!

One day soon, my precious Savior,
what was written in Your Word,
one day soon it will be
the sweetest sounds to be heard.

One day soon, my God of Creation,
all will understand just what it cost.
One day soon, precious Lamb of Calvary,
we will all embrace Your wondrous cross.

One day, yes, one day soon,
though we do not know when,
we will understand how you truly do love us,
ever since our lives began!

As I Look At The Cross

As I look at the cross.
I thought what would I have done?
Would I be yelling "Crucify Him?"
Would I be just like everyone?

Would I be laughing and smiling,
as they put the crown of thorns on His head?
Would I be just like all the others,
or would I stand there grieving instead?

As I look at the cross
and watched His life drain out,
would I understand why He chose to do it,
would I comprehend what it was all about?

Well, the choice is all mine,
just like it is for you, too.
Tell me, my friends as you look at the cross,
do you know what you would do?

When Tears Flowed From the Cross

Good Friday was the day,
so many years ago.
When tears flowed from the cross,
because He loved us so.

It was the Son of God,
that was hanging from that tree.
What hurt Him the most was when He asked,
"My Father, why hast Thou forsaken Me?"

See, He could take all the beatings
and He could bear all the shame.
But what hurt Him the most was being separated
from the Father He loved, as He called out His name.

In this life there will be beatings.
Because of our sins there will be shame.
And we will definitely be separated from God,
unless we call out in Jesus name!

So on this Good Friday,
as we reflect on earth's greatest loss,
remember Sunday and victory is coming,
when tears flowed from the cross.

Do Not Be Distracted

Do not be distracted
as you go about your day.
Stay true to what God has for you,
regardless of what people say.

Keep your focus on Him,
for His purpose for you is right.
Do not be distracted
by this world that's filled with strife.

Wait for His awesome leading,
for He will never lead you wrong.
Read from His Holy Word
and the time won't seem so long.

Do not be distracted,
for many distractions there will surely be.
Pray through the Spirit,
that with open eyes you will always see.

The moral of this poem is
not be distracted as you go along your way.
Just pray, read the Bible and stay focused,
as you wait on Jesus today.

Where Is God

Where is God? People ask,
when they are hurting and confused.
Where is God? He is right there
inside of me and you.

Where is God to answer questions
when this life is so very tough.
Where is God? Where He has always been,
in us, if life is easy or rough.

Where is God? I need Him today
is a cry from so many in pain.
Where is God? He is waiting on us,
to just call out His Holy Name.

See, He wants us all the time,
not for just a day, a month or a year.
He wants your life completely,
so you will know He is always there.

It is not about our hurting,
or the problems we go through.
It is about His love for us
and He wants that also from me and you!

The Fighter

There was a young man, who was fighting a fight,
with cancer, that was consuming him.
Many a prayer went up to heaven above,
saying, "Father, please, let him this battle win!"

A strong healthy man started the fight,
but the battle was taking its toll.
But each day as the battle raged on,
the young man refused to let go.

So as it appeared the enemy was winning,
many thought, "This battle he will not win."
This young man stood strong and kept fighting on,
though his body was getting very thin.

So I got on my knees and started to pray
and said to our Father above,
"How much more must this young man endure?
I know it is not a question of Your love!"

Then the Father spoke to my burdened heart
and said, "It is not about what each one can endure.
It is about how you fight each enemy in sight,
and through Faith each one wins for sure!

So the moral of this poem, please understand,
in this life plenty of battles there will be.
They are won by faith, not by sight,
you are a winner if truly you do believe!

The Loss Of A Loved One

The loss of a loved one
seems more than we can bear,
then Jesus speaks to our hearts and says,
"Don't worry they are here!"

Our hearts ache and hurt
because they are really gone,
then Jesus speaks to our hearts and says,
"They are with Me where they truly belong!"

Our days seem emptier
as we learn to live with our loss,
then Jesus speaks to our hearts and says,
"Life is not over, look to the cross!"

Praise God for our loved ones earthly lives
and the time on earth with us He did give.
Remember it is not about this short earthly life,
but the next, for eternity is where we are meant to live!

Mom's

Moms are Moms
through and through.
They were chosen Moms
for what they do.

They put their children
before themselves,
they perform their duties
better than anyone else.

They nurture, they love,
they teach, they care.
They are Moms forever
that's why God put them here.

And when each day
on this earth is done,
they give praise to Father above,
because He made them a Mom!

Fight On

Our daily battles are many,
the enemy, at times, seems too great.
Then God shouts down from heaven,
"Fight on, for it is never too late."

Whatever the battle you are fighting
and in this life many there will be,
Fight on Christian Soldiers,
for the victory in Jesus you will see.

Don't listen to the enemy
tell you that you cannot win,
pick up your Bible and read,
for in Revelation, it states we win!

God's Word will not change,
so that means it is up to us,
Fight on, fight on, Children of God,
for the victory is in the Cross!!!

Do You Love Me

"Do you love me?" Jesus asked,
when I first awoke from sleep?
"Do you love me more than these,
please, then if you do, Feed My sheep!"

Many, many years ago,
Jesus asked Simon Peter this same question too!
If Jesus asked you today, my friends,
what would you say and do?

Simon Peter replied, in John chapter 21, verse 17,
"Lord, You know all things, You know that I love You!"
My friends, today how are you going to reply to Jesus,
what are the words that will come from you?

For me the answer is always the same
and I pray it will always be,
"Good morning Lord, I love You,
may Your sheep I always be eager to feed!"

Just Let Go

So many Christians today,
still go through the movements for show.
But what they fail to realize is,
they must just let go.

You cannot walk the fence,
with God that cannot be done.
Either you give up your life to Him,
or forever be seeking the Son.

This world has nothing to offer,
that even comes close to Him.
We are here to learn about Him,
then choose for Him to enter in.

So the choice is up to each of us,
in His Word it tells us so.
To have a life in Him,
you must first, "Just let Go!"

Not A Day Worth Living

Pastor's preaching, teachers teaching,
many singing songs to God above.
But what is missing is the commitment
and the surrender of self to His love.

Many a Sunday we go to church
to pray and be free from sin.
But then come the next six days,
for many, it's a life without Him.

Many say they are Christians,
but in truth they do not live.
Their hearts are tied to this earthly world,
their eyes still looking for sin.

My prayer is that one-day they might
understand from His Word what is written.
See, to live a day without Christ, my friends,
is really not a day worth living!

The Day Of Reckoning

The day of reckoning is coming soon,
when we will be judged for what we have done.
Every word spoken, every action taken,
to be reviewed before our God.

It will be too late to ask for forgiveness,
for that time will now have passed.
It will be judgment day for His people,
yes, the day of reckoning at last.

But no one knows when that day will be,
for the Father didn't even tell His beloved Son.
Because of this there still is time,
for there is forgiveness for each and everyone.

Oh, we will be judged for that is true,
but all our wrongs will have been erased.
See, Jesus took the judgment for us,
yes, on Calvary He took our place.

But it is not complete until we ask
and to Him for our sins we do repent.
Then when the day of reckoning comes,
our earthly lives will be viewed as time well spent!

Life's Meaning

Life is full of twists and turns,
sometimes its walls come crashing down.
But if you grab onto Jesus my friends,
life's meaning can truly be found.

Family, friends and life itself,
sometimes overwhelming can surely be.
But once you give your all to Him,
then the Father's Will you will be able to see.

Each life has a purpose,
the reason that only He knows.
But it was created for Him, not us,
yes, for Him and Him alone.

See, what God created in the beginning
will be there forever without end.
He made His choice in the beginning,
now it's up to us, my friends!

How Can I Go Wrong

Another day has come upon us,
we choose what it will be.
Though troubles will be within it,
the outcome is really up to me.

I must choose to be happy,
though from pain my body is not free,
for what is more important than the pain
is knowing that Jesus is living in me.

I must choose to be happy,
though there is sin all around.
My focus must stay on Jesus,
for in Him each day's victory can be found.

So, whatever comes my way today,
because of Jesus I will remain strong,
for in Him I claim each day's happiness,
see, how can I go wrong?

Try Again

A new day is upon you,
and your pain is as strong as before.
You wonder how will I get through?
then, "Try again" is what you hear from the Lord.

You have very little income,
no job seems to be in sight.
Then you hear the Lord say, "Try again",
do not give up for He knows what's right.

Your relationship has failed,
after years of trying to make it work.
"Try Again" the Lord speaks to you,
do not give up, try again with all your worth!

See what is very important,
is to rely just solely on Him.
Do not give up no matter what the trial,
heed His words, "Try again!"

Heading Home

I started heading home today
and paused to look around.
I looked back at some of the memories
that through life's journey
that I have found.

A life full of loving memories
of my wife, family and friends.
A life full of witnessing for Christ,
that made my time
here on earth well spent.

Never compromising the Gospel message
and the truth spoken from His Word.
Never passing an opportunity to pray for others,
for their concerns and needs
are so important to be heard.

So as I kept on heading home
to where with Jesus I knew I had to be.
I thanked the Father above for the time here,
to tell so many of the love
that He has for them and me.

Now it is time for all my Christian brothers and sisters
to be bold and "step up to the plate".
Keep walking closely with the Lord
and tell others of Him,
please, before it is too late!

Love Flows

Love flows from a heart
where it resides within.
It reaches out in Jesus name
and changes all because of Him.

Love flows constantly
and asks nothing in return.
It is because of "choices" we make
and from His Word what we have learned.

Love flows because of Grace,
as a gift that was first given to you.
Once you accept His gift of love,
let it flow to others in all you do.

Love is Jesus, my friends,
either you have Him or you don't.
I pray you choose to love Him today,
for His love will guide you home!

A Fine Line

There is a fine line
between faith and unbelief.
One will bring you courage and hope,
and one will bring you grief.

There is a fine line
between love and also hate.
One will always bring you down,
the other will make you feel great.

There is a fine line
between being empty and being full.
One will always make you feel bad,
the other you will always feel good.

There is a fine line,
it's name is called "choice".
It comes from within the heart
and the Spirit is it's voice.

So "choose" wisely my friends,
whichever it may be,
no eye has seen or ear has heard,
what Jesus has waiting for me.

Steps

Each step in life is but a goal,
taking us to where we ought to be.
"We walk by faith and not by sight"
is what God's Word is saying for all to see.

Put your trust in Him alone
and He will guide your way.
Listen to His Spirit, my friends,
and your steps they will not stray.

Stay in the light of the Son,
as your steps you lay them down.
Keep your focus always on Jesus
though sin is all around.

So as you take another step,
remember this is very true,
your steps will take you somewhere for sure,
where you end up, is up to you!

Trust In Him

The day was dark and dreary,
no sunshine was in sight
I got down on my knees and said,
"God, please make this right!"

I raised my eyes to the Heavens
for just a glimpse I might see,
I needed to feel at that moment
all would be right for me.

Then within the moment,
His Spirit to my heart did speak.
He said, "The answer is in the Word,
there you will find the answers that you seek".

So I opened up my Bible,
and to Philippians 4:6 I did read,
"Do not be anxious about anything"
is what my eyes did see.

Then I did read further,
"in everything by prayer and supplication"
is what it said,
and "with thanksgiving, let your requests
be made known to God",
see, this is what God was trying to get into my head.

Remember dark days will come,
but Son-light there will always be.
So don't worry about anything my friends,
trust in Him and His Word,
that's what He was saying to me.

The Empty Swing

As I walked by a playground
I noticed an empty swing.
My mind went back to my childhood
and the happiness the swing did bring.

I remembered just learning how to do it
and when I couldn't, being pushed from behind.
I remembered soaring up to the Heavens,
yes, the empty swing brought that back to mind.

Then I thought of the swing being empty
and no laughter or singing did I hear.
I thought of a childhood now past,
now living in a world of doubt and fear.

So the next time you pass a playground
and you don't know what the next minute will bring,
it doesn't matter how old you are,
just look for the empty swing.

Sit down and forget your problems,
reach out to the Heavens and begin to sing,
laugh and keep on laughing, my friends,
and thank God for the empty swing!

What Are You Waiting For

So many people just like me
are waited for something, what could it be?
The things of this world just couldn't do
and the One you need is waiting for me and you.

No matter what we have or what we don't,
it truly doesn't matter and truly won't.
See, only Jesus can satisfy the need
and it won't be satisfied unless you believe.

So each day will come and each day will pass
and the need will be there just like the last.
Some days you may win but most you will lose,
see it all comes down to what you choose.

For me I chose Jesus, He is the Word and my Light,
now living each day makes everything right!
So if you are still searching each day like before,
my question to you is, "What are you waiting for?"

There Will Come A Time

There will come a time,
I know not when,
you will be called to God,
be prepared, my friends.

There will come a time,
I know it's true,
for it happened to me
and I know will happen to you.

For He is our Creator,
you can believe this or not.
Yes, Jesus His Son,
did die on the Cross.

He died for a reason
so that no one would lose,
there will come a time my, friends,
you will have to choose.

See, you cannot wait
till the end to make your choice,
it must be made now
and be made with your voice.

Yes, there will come a time,
God is waiting for you.
He already made His choice,
what are you going to choose?

Jesus Has My Back

My body is being attacked,
no peace can I find.
Even in my solitude,
the enemy invades my mind.

Where can I find relief?
Which way do I turn?
Where will my help come from?
What is it I must learn?

Then I opened my Bible,
Psalm 121, I started to read.
"My help comes from the Lord",
is what it said to me.

No matter what is against me.
No matter how severe the attack.
What I read from the Bible is
"Jesus has my back!!!!"

Grab Onto Him

I was up on top of the mountain
and said, "I really like it here."
For on top of the mountain
the air felt so clean and God so very near.

Everything seemed to be brighter,
I could see all around.
I didn't have any cares,
I really didn't want to go back down.

For now in the valley
it is different as can be.
Darkness is just about everywhere,
so many problems for all you see.

But what these two have in common,
not many can understand.
See, whichever one you happen to be,
you will find God's outstretched hand.

So praise Him in the good times,
yes, praise Him in the bad.
Make sure to grab onto Him,
you will be glad you had.

When It Rains It Pours

When it rains it pours
is what they say.
Sometimes our problems are few,
sometimes they never go away.

Problems like raindrops,
may just sprinkle down.
Then all of a sudden,
there is no relief to be found.

But God in all His mercy,
knew troubles like rain there would be.
That is why, my friends, He cries out,
"Please, just believe in Me!"

See, He will shelter us in the downpours.
He will keep us dry with His Word.
His Gospel message assures us of that,
what a message that is to be heard.

Every Morning

Every morning when I first awake,
I thank my Lord, who is my life, and my love.
For He has given me another day
to serve Him from above.

He has granted me this day
to be His hands, His feet and His Word.
To share with others that have not known,
the sweetest Gospel ever heard.

To help the needy and the poor,
to help heal the broken hearts.
To share His love with all I meet,
as He did with me, from the start.

See, the reason He has granted me
this day in which I'm here to live,
is because it is how on this earth
He can still reach the lost and still give.

Yes, give the gift of Salvation,
that through His grace we all can receive.
For through that special gift is also found
Deliverance, health, prosperity, if only you'd believe.

God U R 4 Me

I picked up the telephone
and dialed "God U R 4 Me"
On the other end I heard,
"Yes my child, what do you want from Me?"

I said, "Lord, I have many friends,
that I want for You to bless.
See, sometimes no matter what we do
our lives can become such a mess.

I want for You to touch my friends
and never leave their side.
Please give them love and comfort
that only You can provide.

Let them know I love them so
and share this love through You.
And also may I make one more request?
Would You bless their families, too?

Well, Thank You for Your time Lord,
for You're always ready to hear my call.
Just one more thing I want to say,
Lord, I love You most of all!"

Life's Many Obstacles

I came upon one of life's many obstacles,
I said, "Lord, how can this be?
It is not letting me continue,
to do what You ask of me.

What can I say, what can I do
to clear it from my path?
How can I remove this obstacle
that is keeping me from my task?"

Then within the moment,
in my heart the Lord did speak.
He said, "Look closely at this obstacle
for in it you will find Me.

See, life's many obstacles
are put there by choice.
You will learn, grow and get stronger,
and be always listening for my voice.

You will hear Me say, have patience.
You will hear Me say, have no fear.
You should not be looking at it as an obstacle,
but why I brought you here."

So the moral of this poem,
in life, many obstacles there will be.
It is not about the obstacle,
but that it brings you closer to God, you see!

The Final Battle

The fighter entered the arena,
the final battle was at stake.
His body was weak and beaten,
no more he could give or take

Though it appeared to many who watched,
this battle he could not win.
But God looked down from the heavens
and said, "Yes, today's battle you will surely win!

For you have fought every battle
that on earth was given you.
You never gave up fighting,
for there is no quit in you.

Though many battles on earth are present,
some more severe than all the rest.
It is in the final earthly battle
where you truly showed your best.

So welcome home, brave fighter,
no more battles will there be.
You have fought the good fight,
now you belong here with Me!"

Why Not You

I have seen so many people
lost, hurting and confused.
Then as I looked at my life,
I wondered why I did not lose.

So many people hurting,
their bodies filled with pain.
Then as I looked at my life,
I wondered why it wasn't the same?

Then within a heartbeat
my life changed like I've never known.
Pain was ever present within
and fear within me had grown.

I cried out to the Heavens,
"Lord, why is this happening to me?
I am now one of the hurting,
Lord, please tell me how can this be?"

Then within the moment,
I became quiet through and through.
The answered rang from above,
"My Child, why not you?

You are no different
than any Child of Mine,
in this life you will all have problems,
see it is only a question of time.

So remember to live each day
the very best you can,
and remember I am with you always,
yes, in the good as well as the bad."

In Just A Moment

In just a moment a life can change
for either the good or the bad.
In just a moment you would wish
you didn't do what you had.

In just a moment you can change life
from just a word that is said.
In just a moment you can scar someone,
carrying that scar through their life ahead.

So let us stop before that moment comes,
let us think of what it would do.
Will it be a moment to lift someone up
or take them lower before you are through?

Let first give a moment to God,
yes, even before we speak.
See, in just a moment He will guide us,
if only His wisdom we do seek!

He Is There

I didn't have an envelope
to put my offering in.
I didn't have a hymn book,
so to Him I could sing.

I didn't have a Bible
to understand His Word.
I just sat in silence wondering,
how can I be heard?

He told my heart be patient
and to bow my head in prayer.
He told me to believe in Him
with all my heart, for He will always be there.

So the moral of this poem, my friends,
though with your eyes you cannot see.
Know He will always be there,
just like I know He is for me.

Lord, What Can I Do For You

I got up this morning and said,
"Lord, what can I do for You?"
He said, "My child, I am not the one in need,
but look for others and see what you can do.

Be My feet to bring them food,
be My hands to hold them tight,
be My mouth to speak the Word
to let them know everything will be all right.

Be My ears to hear them cry,
be My eyes to see their pain,
let them know that I am there,
with them every step of the way.

So many that are in need,
so many that still just don't see.
Show them what I am like, My child,
that's what you can do for Me."

How Do I Believe

How do I believe someone asked,
in a God I cannot see?
How can I be sure
that God really loves me?

How can I know,
when in trouble He is really there?
How can I be rest assured
that God really cares?

Well, for me the answer is simple,
all you have to do is open your eyes.
Look all around and see
where all His beauty lies.

Open up His Word
that hasn't changed since day one.
Listen to all His praises
from hymns that are being sung.

Then ask any believer,
that loves Him with all their heart.
They truly understand there is a God,
who loved us from the start.

I Want More Of Jesus

I want more of Jesus,
I just can't get enough.
I really try to fill up the most
when this life gets tough.

I want more of Jesus,
my heart cries out for more.
Once you feel His presence,
you want more than the day before.

I want more of Jesus,
for that is how my life is now.
Ever since I surrendered to Him,
I have that hunger in me somehow.

I want more of Jesus,
I pray you feel the way I do.
Jesus is what I live for,
He is what gets me through!

What Would You Pay

What would you give
what would you pay,
to have eternal peace,
and be free every day?

What would this cost
each one of us today?
What would you give?
What would you pay?

What could you do
to achieve all this?
What could be done
to insure eternal bliss?

Well, nothing you can do
and nothing you can pay
can give you all or
any of this today.

But don't be discouraged
and please don't lose heart.
For God in His awesome wisdom
had all this planned from the start.

You see, God had a way
to insure no one would lose.
For through His Son, Jesus,
all we had to do, was choose.

Just ask Him to forgive you
for the sins you have done,
and ask Him to be your Lord and Savior,
all because of the Son.

For everything is waiting for us
and will be there on judgment day.
For you see it was all paid by Jesus
and there is no other way!

Jesus Came to My House

Jesus came to my house
He knocked and said, "Hi, there's three!
My Father, Me the Son and the Holy Spirit"
Yes, it was, the Trinity you see.

They came because they knew they were welcomed
and here peace and love was found.
But they were unsure of the other homes,
close by in our hometown.

Jesus said, "You see your neighbors every day.
Did you ever mention Me?
Did you ever tell them about anyone of Us?
Did you ever mention the Trinity?"

Jesus said, "Which house should we go to next?
Can you tell Us where We should go?
There are so many homes We want to visit,
and tell them We love them so!"

I said, "Lord I am so ashamed,
for it is with only other Christians do I speak.
For I am always unsure what to say,
to all the non-believers, the sick and the weak.

They All smiled and touched my hand
and said, "Well, it is time that We should go."
But the Holy Spirit said, "I will stay here with you,
because you love Us so!"

He said to God the Father and Jesus His beloved Son,
"I will stay here in this house
to help guide others along.
Yes, I will stay in this house,
for it is here that I belong!

I will choose the words to say,
for non-believers we will seek,
We will minister to the sick,
and give strength to the weak.

And one day We will all be together again,
when our work here on earth is done,
singing praises to God the Father
and Jesus, His beloved Son!"

A Welcome And A Smile

I walked into a church today
where the people seemed to smile.
Through no one seemed to notice me
I thought I would stay a while.

A lot of people seemed friendly
but just let me be.
I thought maybe if I just sat still
that someone would come to me.

Good music started playing,
some of the songs seemed like they cared,
but for most that sat near by
they just looked, some even stared.

My heart cried out I am here,
please someone come and say hi.
I came here today
for reasons I don't know why.

Lately I felt all alone
just helpless as can be.
My heart said go inside this church today
for someone is waiting for me.

Before the time was over
and all were walking out,
someone grabbed my hand and said "Welcome"
I saw you come in but didn't want to shout.

My name is Jesus
and I have been waiting for you.
There are times I came here also
and felt neglected too!

So please come back next time,
for it might take these people a while,
for them to understand it isn't hard,
it just takes a "welcome!" and a smile.

The Pastor

God spoke to the Pastor's heart
and said, "Go teach them about Me!"
So this man, who was called by God,
set out to teach, so all would see.

He came to a group of people
that appeared to be all lost.
He opened up his Bible and said,
"Let me teach you about the Cross!"

Some just look dumbfounded
as he began to speak.
Some just shook their heads
and said, "This is for the weak!"

So onward he went
and more people he did find,
he opened up his Bible and said,
"Jesus healed the blind!"

But like the people before them,
they just couldn't see
what this man of God was talking about,
most said, "It's just not for me!"

So the Pastor knelt down and prayed,
"Lord, to You I want to please!"
What am I doing wrong,
is it something about me?"

The Lord spoke to his heart and said,
"You are doing just what I asked,
your love for Me is greater
than any of these tasks!

When you speak they are hearing,
keep showing your love and Mine.
For most the seed has been planted,
now it just takes time!"

My Thoughts

I went to a wake yesterday,
for a family that lost their son.
As I left the funeral home I thought
their sorrow has just begun.

I thought of a lot of seniors,
in nursing homes, feeling lost and in despair.
Each one's face seem to be saying,
please tell me, why am I living here?

I thought of all the people,
with no job and nothing to eat.
So many whose lives have now changed,
homeless and living in the streets.

Then I thought of the many
fighting addictions every day.
And also those with mental and physical problems,
how do they make it through the day?

I raised my head above and asked God,
"Why must this all be?"
God touched my heart and said,
"It's called life, a time to learn about Me.

Shortly ***this*** life will be over,
yes, no more sorrow, no more pain.
There will be no memory of it,
for it will all be erased in My Son's Name!

So please stay focused, child of Mine,
as this life on earth goes on.
Remember to tell all you see about Me,
and of the Spirit, and Jesus My loving Son.

See, one day all will know
and will truly understand.
Just as it was written in My Word,
there is a place called Heaven, yes, a Promised Land."

Jesus Is The Way

Jesus looked down from the Cross
and saw the world
as we made it to be,
with the blood flowing
from the crown of thorns.
He saw all the world wars,
Hiroshima and Nagasaki.

As the soldiers spear pierced His side,
He heard the cries
from so many still to come.
From the Jewish people
in the concentration camps,
to the many people around the world
being killed, one by one.

As the breath was leaving His body,
He saw that 9/11
was on its way.
He raised His eyes
and looked above and said,
"Father please
forgive them all today!"

See, Jesus knew
what was going to happen,
and the Father believed
and loves His Son.
His Spirit was sent here to teach us,
the victory is not of this world,
but in Heaven that it is won!

So wars will come
and wars will go
and for many, they will pay the price.
But what is most important
is God's love,
that was proved
through His sacrifice!

So if you truly believe that,
then the gospel message
will truly set you free,
tell someone about John 14:6 in the Bible
where Jesus said,
"I am the Way, the Truth, and the Life;
no one comes to the Father but by Me."

Use this page to list your favorite poems with their page number!